BIONIC T1D

Nina Wadia

Illustrated by
Nanette Regan

RISING ★ STARS

ISBN: 9781510477254

Text © 2019 Nina Wadia
Illustrations, design and layout © 2019 Rising Stars UK Ltd
First published in 2019 by Rising Stars UK Ltd

Rising Stars UK Ltd, part of Hodder Education Group
An Hachette UK Company
Carmelite House, 50 Victoria Embankment, London, EC4Y 0DZ

www.risingstars-uk.com

Impression number 10 9 8 7 6 5 4 3 2 1
Year 2023 2022 2021 2020 2019

Author: Nina Wadia
Series Editor: Sasha Morton
Publisher: Helen Parker
Illustrator: Nanette Regan/Bright Group International
Character concepts: Tia and Aidan Mirza
Educational Consultant: Pauline Allen
Design concept: Helen Townson
Page layout: Lorraine Inglis
Senior Editor: Kirsten Taylor

With thanks to the Type 1 Diabetes charity JDRF UK for expert information and advice.

With thanks to the schools that took part in the development of *Reading Planet* KS2, including: Ancaster CE Primary School, Ancaster; Downsway Primary School, Reading; Ferry Lane Primary School, London; Foxborough Primary School, Slough; Griffin Park Primary School, Blackburn; St Barnabas CE First & Middle School, Pershore; Tranmoor Primary School, Doncaster; and Wilton CE Primary School, Wilton

A catalogue record for this title is available from the British Library

Printed in the United Kingdom

Orders: Please contact Bookpoint Ltd, 130 Park Drive, Milton Park, Abingdon, Oxon OX14 4SE. Telephone: (44) 01235 400555. Email primary@bookpoint.co.uk

CONTENTS

HORRID HOLIDAY

I will never forget my first day in Year 3. Not because I was nervous about going back to school. Not because I hadn't seen some of my friends for six weeks. And not even because I'd heard that there were some scarily strict new teachers. It was because I had changed, in the most unexpected way.

My name is Bionic T1D. That wasn't always my name. I used to be called Maverick: Maverick Masters (just like Bruce Banner before he turned into the Hulk!).

I have a big sister, Madeline, and a little brother, Mickey. I'm sure you've worked out that my parents' favourite letter in the world is 'M'. (Their names are Michael and Melanie!) This is the story of how I (almost) became a superhero ...

It all started during the summer holidays. I had strange pains in my stomach and I felt angry all the time – just like the Hulk!

5

I felt tired all the time, too. And worst of all, I was always thirsty. No matter how much water I drank, I still needed more. I wondered if I had sprung a leak somewhere, because I just couldn't figure out where all that water was going.

6

Then one morning, things got much worse. I felt very dizzy and as if I was going to be sick. I called out to Madeline, because her room is closest to mine.

When she saw me lying down on the bed all curled up in a ball, she frowned. She said I looked really grey and weird, and ran to get Mum and Dad. Then Mickey came into the room and wanted to play with me and got all upset because I could barely move.

Mum and Dad rushed to my room. They took one look at me and knew something was terribly wrong. My dad picked me up, put me in the back of the car and we all hurried to our doctor.

Madeline was actually very nice to me (for once!) and stroked my hair, while Mickey made funny noises to make me laugh, but I could barely manage a smile.

My sister and brother had to sit in the waiting area, while Mum and Dad and I were taken into the doctor's surgery.

Dr Wassouf asked my parents loads of questions and started tapping around my tummy. Then he took some blood from my finger, put it onto a stick and placed it into a machine.

We seemed to be waiting forever, until we heard the machine make a long blaring beep. Dr Wassouf then took out the stick and looked at it. Immediately, his eyes opened really wide. He looked at my mum and dad and said, "Oh my. It would seem that Maverick is Type 1."

Huh?

2
PANCREATIC PANIC

My mum was so nervous she just said blankly, "Type 1 what?"

"Type 1 Diabetic," the doctor explained. "Or T1D as my other young patients like to call it. Maverick has Type 1 Diabetes."

Although my dad seemed calm, my mum looked shocked. I thought she was going to cry! I wasn't sure what this meant, but

I knew something had definitely changed in my life. I suddenly felt really scared.

"It's okay," Dr Wassouf continued. "Please don't be alarmed. The good news is, Type 1 Diabetes can be managed very well once you understand it and know what you are doing. We'll teach you everything you need to know."

But there was silence in the room.

"Millions of people all over the world have it!" he continued, trying to keep our spirits up.

Then, Dr Wassouf turned to me and asked, "Maverick, do you understand what's going on?"

I shook my head, looking down at my feet.

"Well," he said kindly. "Let me explain it simply. In your tummy, you have something called a pancreas. The pancreas helps your body digest your food by pumping out something called insulin. This helps to convert your food into energy, so you can run around all day. Your pancreas, however, has decided to go on strike – for good."

"Does that mean I can't ever eat again?!" I panicked.

"Ha, no young man," Dr Wassouf chuckled gently. "Quite the opposite. You can eat anything you like! It just means, that we have to find another way of getting that insulin into you."

"Can I still play football?" I asked, secretly crossing my fingers behind my back.

"Of course you can. In fact, any kind of exercise would be very good for you."

Yes! I exclaimed in my head.

"In fact, there won't be anything you can't do because of Type 1. Did you know that there are Olympic champions who have T1D?"

"No way!" I said, louder than I had intended.

"Yes way!" replied Dr Wassouf, smiling widely.

He then paused for a moment, leaned towards me and said, "Maverick, do you like gadgets?"

3

HYPOS AND HYPERS

I felt really poorly over the next few days and weeks as we tried to work out how much of that insulin stuff I needed.

We went back and forth to the hospital, meeting all kinds of doctors and nurses, and even a psychologist! (That's someone you can talk to about how you feel about everything that's happening to you.) I also met other kids with T1D, just like me, and I even made a few new friends.

This wasn't how I thought I'd be spending my school holidays, though. Some days I felt a bit fed up. I didn't want people to know how my life had changed over the summer. I had never heard of T1D before, and I was scared that they might treat me differently, or not want to play with me. Maybe they wouldn't even want to be friends with me anymore.

Although everyone at home was being really nice to me, it was slowly sinking in that every time I wanted to eat something, I would have to inject myself with insulin. You see, it just plain hurt! And also, I was hugely embarrassed at having to pull my  trousers down on one side, as my thigh was the best place for the needle to go! Madeline and Mickey let me choose what we had for dinner every night to try and cheer me up. (It did a little bit.)

I also had to carry a kitbag around with me everywhere I went from now on. I had to check it every morning and make sure it had my insulin pen, my lancet (Mickey called it

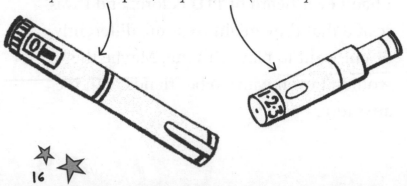

my finger pricker!), my blood sugar measuring machine, strips to go in the machine and some super-fast-acting sugar tablets for emergencies.

It was a real pain having to carry all this around, but it did have one good thing in it – a snack bar! Any kind I liked, even with pieces of chocolate in it!

The worst thing was that sometimes, if I didn't eat enough, I would have something called a hypo. Hypos made me feel awful because I'd go pale, get sweaty and feel dizzy. If I didn't eat some food with sugar in it straight away, I would even pass out.

On the other hand, when I ate too much sugary food – like a huge piece of Mickey's birthday cake – without injecting enough insulin, I would have a hyper. That would then make me feel really sick! It was a lot to remember.

In the meantime, my parents had to tell everyone in our family the news. They had all been wondering why they hadn't seen us over the summer. My dad had also been super-busy working out a plan with the headteacher and my class teachers for my return to school in September. I wasn't sure if I was ready to go back to school, but I realised I had to. There was just one thing left to do, which terrified me. I had to tell my friends.

***

So, there we were. First day back at school and I hadn't dared say a word to anyone yet. I really liked the feeling that nothing had changed.

It was morning break. Dad had packed me a banana for my morning snack, but I was so busy playing football with my mates that I had forgotten to eat it.

19

"Come on Mav! Kick the ball to me, I'm free!" shouted Ralph.

"I'm trying!" I yelled back. I was completely out of breath but I kicked the ball as hard as I could.

I had kicked it too wide. The ball whizzed past Mr Barker, just missing his face. We all stopped short and gasped. Mr Barker was friendly enough, but he had quite a temper! He got especially cross about rough games in the playground at break time.

"Sorry, Mr Barker!" I squealed. Just then, the bell went and I ran back to the main building as fast as I could, followed by my friends.

When we got to the foot of the staircase that led up to our classroom, I suddenly felt dizzy. I realised that I hadn't had a big enough breakfast to give me the energy I needed for playing football. And then I remembered that I didn't eat that banana before running around either!

"Oh no, please don't faint!" I whispered to myself. But it was too late.

4
DAY ONE DISASTER

I was resting in the medical room when Tim, Ralph and Limkosa came looking for me. An hour ago, my body felt weak and my head felt cloudy. My legs seemed very heavy, too, like someone was sitting on them. I was feeling a lot better now because of the glucose tablets I'd taken and was even getting ready to go for lunch. But suddenly Tim pushed open the door before Ms Lee (who was looking after me) could stop him.

"You okay, Mav—?" But before he could even finish saying my name, he gasped.

They couldn't take their eyes off the needle in my thigh ... and I was the one holding it!

"Er … what's going on, Ms Lee?!" croaked Ralph.

"It's alright, children. Maverick knows what he's doing," she said gently. "We've measured his blood sugar and he's fine now to inject some insulin before he eats his lunch."

I could feel my face turning red and there was utter silence. That was, until Ralph said, "Cool! Can I try injecting myself, too?!"

ABSOLUTELY NOT!

shrieked Ms Lee.

And then a moment later, we all burst out laughing!

"Are you coming back to class soon?" asked Limkosa hopefully.

"He will once I've scanned him," replied Ms Lee.

"Scanned him?!" the three of them gasped together.

Ms Lee smiled and without saying another word, turned up my shirt sleeve and there it was, my little secret gadget, a sensor. A white, shiny disc stuck to my arm that told me what my blood sugar level was.

"Whoa! Stop the press!" Ralph exclaimed.

'Stop the press' was Ralph's favourite phrase. It was something reporters used to say when there was a big story to put on the front page of a newspaper. There was lots of 'oohing' and 'aahing' as I showed them my scanner. The number on the scanner was now at seven.

Seven was good. ✓

Two point nine, which was what my blood sugar level had been when I staggered into the medical room, was bad! ✗

"Well, come on then, Bionic!" said Ralph. "You've always wanted to be a superhero – now you've got that gadget on your arm, I guess you really are one! I bet you can't wait to show it to everyone. I wish I had a one too!"

I suddenly felt excited. Ralph was right. I was Bionic! Bionic T1D!

"Race you to the lunch room!" I shouted, laughing, as I bolted past the three of them, faster than lightning!

5
FANTASTIC FAMILY AND FRIENDS

Over the next few weeks at school, I felt better and better about living with my T1D. It was actually really great not to have to hide it. In fact, when people stared at the white sensor disc on my arm, I told them all kinds of funny stories. My favourite one was that I was an alien who was gathering information to send back to my home planet, Theta. They would look at me all shocked and confused, and then my friends and I would burst out laughing!

Sometimes, other people had fun with my diabetes. Once, I was too busy playing video games to listen to what Melanie was saying. She pressed the sensor on my arm and said, "Hello, anybody home?!" and, again, we all laughed.

I did like to think I had superpowers for real, too. Who else would be able to track down the school hamster when she escaped from her cage? Nobody had seen Maisie all day, but then Limkosa spotted her during our French lesson.

"Look, Mav," she whispered. "Maisie's on top of the bookshelf!"

Getting her back was a job for Bionic T1D! My plan was to leap from table to table across the classroom to reach her. Unfortunately, Madame Couderre didn't like that plan at all. As soon as I put my foot on my chair, she shouted at me to sit down before I had an accident.

Even more unfortunately, Maisie didn't seem to like it when Madame Couderre shouted. She ran off the end of the bookshelf in fright and landed in Madame Couderre's lap. At least Maisie was safe – even if it wasn't quite the superhero rescue I had in mind!

Funnily enough, I had another chance to carry out an animal rescue when our neighbour's cat got stuck in their tree. This time, I climbed like Spider-Man to chase Fluffy down. Except then I got stuck in the tree's branches and Dad had to get a ladder to bring me down.

There was also that time I was helping Mum water the garden and pretending the hose was my secret superhero weapon – except I got myself all tangled in it and ended up soaking wet. (Talk about embarrassing!)

I don't think Mickey and Mum will ever let me forget it! Being a superhero is definitely harder than it looks.

So, although my new nickname is Bionic T1D, my T1D hasn't changed how my family and friends feel about me at all. We still do everything together, just like we did before, only, between you and me, I do it a little bit better and a little bit faster!

Now answer the questions ...

1 What happened in the first chapter of the story?

2 Why do you think Dr Wassouf tried to cheer everyone up when he realised what was wrong with Mav and which sentence suggests this didn't work?

3 Can you explain why Mav worried about telling his friends that he has Type 1 Diabetes? Give two reasons, using examples from the text to help you.

4 Reread pages 19–21 and sum up what happened to Mav on his first day back at school.

5 Which word could the author have used instead of 'shrieked' in the sentence '"ABSOLUTELY NOT!" shrieked Ms Lee.'?

6 What did Mav describe as his 'secret gadget'?

7 How do Mav's feelings about his diabetes change once his friends know about it?

8 Which of Mav's adventures as Bionic T1D did you like the best?